FOND DU LAC PUBLIC LIBRARY

D1256231

Pebble® Plus

I Want a Pet

I Want a Dog

by Kimberly M. Hutmacher

Consulting Editor: Gail Saunders-Smith, PhD

Consultant: Jennifer Zablotny, DVM
Member, American Veterinary Medical Association

CAPSTONE PRESS
a capstone imprint

Pebble Plus is published by Capstone Press,
1710 Roe Crest Drive, North Mankato, Minnesota 56003.
www.capstonepub.com

Books published by Capstone Press are manufactured with paper containing at least 10 percent post-consumer waste.

Library of Congress Cataloging-in-Publication Data
Hutmacher, Kimberly.
 I want a dog / by Kimberly M. Hutmacher.
   p. cm.—(Pebble plus. i want a pet)
 Includes bibliographical references and index.
 Summary: "Simple text and full-color photographs describe the responsibilities involved in caring for and choosing a dog as a pet"—Provided by publisher.
  ISBN 978-1-4296-7595-6 (library binding)
 1. Dogs--Juvenile literature. I. Title.
 SF426.5.H88 2012
 636.7—dc23   2011021650

Editorial Credits
Erika L. Shores, editor; Bobbie Nuytten, designer; Sarah Schuette, photo stylist; Marcy Morin, studio scheduler;
   Kathy McColley, production specialist

Photo Credits
All images by Capstone Studio/Karon Dubke, except Shutterstock: Joy Brown, cover (top left), Waldemar Dabrowski,
   cover (top right)

Note to Parents and Teachers

The I Want a Pet series supports common core state standards for English language arts related to reading informational text. This book describes and illustrates dog ownership. The images support early readers in understanding the text. The repetition of words and phrases helps early readers learn new words. This book also introduces early readers to subject-specific vocabulary words, which are defined in the Glossary section. Early readers may need assistance to read some words and to use the Table of Contents, Glossary, Read More, Internet Sites, and Index sections of the book.

Printed in the United States of America in North Mankato, Minnesota.

102011   006405CGS12

Table of Contents

Dogs Are for Me

Who can resist the wagging tail

and friendly lick of a dog?

Let's find out just what

it takes to have a dog

for a pet.

My Responsibilities

You'll care for your dog each day. You'll take it for walks and play fetch. All dogs need exercise and lots of attention.

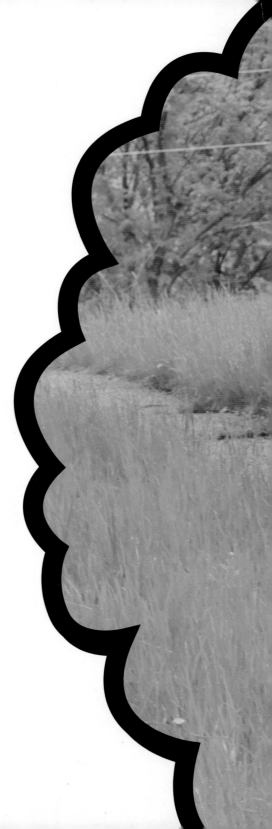

You'll be expected to feed
your furry friend
and give it fresh water.
Most dogs eat twice a day.

Young pups must learn

to go to the bathroom outside.

You'll have to housebreak a puppy.

Don't forget you'll need to

clean up accidents.

Plan to read books on how
to teach your pooch
good manners. You can also
take your dog to classes
that teach obedience.

Picking Your Pooch

Think you're ready for

the responsibility?

Find the perfect pooch for you.

Adopt a dog from a shelter

or buy one from a breeder.

Time to shop! You'll spend
money on a leash, collar,
and tags. Don't forget
food, bowls, a brush,
and a bed.

Take your new dog to
a veterinarian to make sure
it's healthy. Your dog will also
need a yearly checkup
and vaccinations.

With good care and tons of love,

dogs can live up to 15 years.

Choose a happy

and playful pooch!

It will be a great friend.

Glossary

breeder—a person who raises animals to sell

housebreak—to teach a dog to go to the bathroom outdoors

manners—polite behavior; dogs should learn to sit, stay, and come when called

obedience—to follow rules and commands

responsibility—a duty or a job

shelter—a safe place where lost or homeless pets can stay

vaccination—a shot of medicine that protects animals from a disease

veterinarian—a doctor who treats sick or injured animals; veterinarians also help animals stay healthy

Read More

Adams, Michelle Medlock. *Care for a Puppy.* A Robbie Reader. Hockessin, Del.: Mitchell Lane, 2010.

Armentrout, David and Patricia Armentrout. *Doggie Duties.* Let's Talk about Pets. Vero Beach, Fla.: Rourke Publishing, 2011.

Stevens, Kathryn. *Dogs.* Pet Care For Kids. Mankato, Minn.: The Child's World, 2009.

Internet Sites

FactHound offers a safe, fun way to find Internet sites related to this book. All of the sites on FactHound have been researched by our staff.

Here's all you do:

Visit *www.facthound.com*

Type in this code: 9781429675956

Check out projects, games and lots more at
www.capstonekids.com

Index

Word Count: 208
Grade: 1
Early-Intervention Level: 14